Snow Leopard Kingdom

A Coloring Book of the Elusive and Endangered Cats

This book belong to

____

____

Welcome to Snow Leopard Kingdom, a coloring book featuring the majestic and elusive snow leopard. This beautiful and endangered species is one of the world's most fascinating and enigmatic animals, inhabiting the rugged mountains of Central Asia.

The pages of this coloring book take you on a journey through the snow leopard's kingdom, showcasing the beauty and complexity of its natural habitat. From the icy peaks of the Himalayas to the rocky slopes of the Altai Mountains, you'll discover the snow leopard's world and the creatures that share it.

Each page features a unique theme of the snow leopards in their natural habitat . Whether you're an animal lover, a coloring enthusiast, or simply looking for a relaxing activity, Snow Leopard Kingdom offers a chance to connect with this amazing species and learn more about its conservation.

With intricate illustrations and detailed information about the snow leopard's habitat, behavior, and conservation status, this coloring book provides a fun and educational experience for all ages. By coloring these pages, you'll not only create beautiful artwork but also help raise awareness about the need to protect this elusive and endangered cat.

So grab your pencils, markers, or paints and join us on a journey through the Snow Leopard Kingdom.

The Snow Leopard : All you need to know

Snow Leopards are large, solitary cats that inhabit the mountains of Central Asia, including the Himalayas, the Altai Mountains, and the Tibetan Plateau. They are highly adapted to their high-altitude habitat, with thick fur, large paws, and a long tail that helps them balance on steep, rocky terrain.

Snow Leopards are known for their elusive nature and are rarely seen in the wild. They are primarily nocturnal and hunt for prey, including wild sheep and goats, in the early morning or late evening hours. They are also opportunistic hunters, and will eat smaller animals like rodents and birds if larger prey is scarce.

Snow Leopards are sometimes called the "ghost of the mountain" due to their elusive nature and their ability to blend in with their surroundings. Their white-gray fur provides excellent camouflage in snowy environments, and their silent, stealthy movements make them difficult to spot. They are also known for their haunting calls, which echo through the mountains and contribute to their ghostly reputation.

Snow Leopards dwell in rocky areas, where they use their powerful legs and paws to climb and navigate steep terrain. They are well-adapted to cold temperatures and high elevations, with thick fur and a large nasal cavity that warms and moistens the air they breathe. They also have large lungs and a strong heart, which helps them cope with the low oxygen levels at high altitude.

Snow Leopards reproduce sexually, with females typically giving birth to a litter of 2-3 cubs after a gestation period of around 90-100 days. Cubs are born blind and helpless and are cared for by their mother for the first 18-22 months of their lives. Snow Leopards reach sexual maturity at around 2-3 years of age and have a lifespan of around 10-12 years in the wild.

Unfortunately, Snow Leopards are listed as a vulnerable species by the International Union for Conservation of Nature (IUCN) due to habitat loss, poaching, and retaliatory killing by farmers who view them as a threat to their livestock. It is estimated that there are only around 4,000-6,500 Snow Leopards left in the wild.

Conservation efforts are underway to protect Snow Leopards and their habitat. These include anti-poaching measures, community-based conservation programs, and efforts to reduce human-wildlife conflict. Snow Leopard conservation is also an important part of the conservation of their mountain ecosystem, which provides crucial resources like water and timber to millions of people in the region.

In addition to being an important symbol of the fragile beauty of high-altitude ecosystems, Snow Leopards also have cultural significance in the region. They are revered by many indigenous communities, who view them as guardians of the mountains and spiritual beings.